Where Grasses Bend

Poems from Portland
to Steens Mountain
in the time of Plagues

By
Mimi German

my witness is the empty sky

Jack Kerouac

PUBLISH

EYEPUBLISHEWE
PUBLISHING POETRY, LITERATURE, ART, MUSIC
FOR HUMANITY'S SAKE
A BRAND NEW PUBLISHING COMPANY
SAN FRANCISCO
FOUNDED 2020

For
all the desert beings

Acknowledgments

The Scenic View was published in Remembering Jack Kerouac On His 100th Birthday by the National Beat Poetry Foundation in 2022

Barking At Crows was published in Sublunary Review, 2022
A Thousand Grains of Sand was published in International Times in 2022

A Thousand Grains of Sand published in the Long Island Quarterly in 2022

Poverty was published in the New Generation Beats 2022 Anthology by the National Beat Poetry Foundation and in International Times in 2022

Table of Contents

Acknowledgments ii

Table of Contents iii

PART 1..1

March 2020 3

As They Count The Dead 4

Dusk...5

Containment...6

I Cannot Sleep 7

Inside This Abyss..8

Sea Winds...9

Resembling A Dead Weed 10

Time Immeasurable...11

Indigo 12

Adrift 13

Inside 14

Love In The Hours..15

Fallen Fruit...16

The Dark Bird 17

Where Once A Jackal Walked...18

Hope 20

Searching For Air..21

In June, I Have Only Questions..22

Thirst 23

Burning Prayers...24

Light Years 26

Still Life 27

I Surrender 28

Thoughts While Weeding During the Plague 30

Fermentation 32

The Eighth Month 33

When The Ceiling Cracks 34

Morning Prayer 35

Of Love 36

PART II 39

In This State 41

The Scenic View 42

Barking At Crows 44

A Thousand Grains of Sand 46

Poverty 47

Apparition On a Park Bench 48

The Weight of Rain 49

9833 N. Willamette Blvd 50

Ferlinghetti's Interruption 52

Rosh Hashanah 5783 54

The Women Screamed 55

About That Toilet on Lombard 56

In America the Beautiful 58

On the Bridge 59

Walking The Slope 60

War 61

United States 62

v

Joy 63

The Teapot 64

Night...65

After the Protests..66

Martyrs...67

I Kali 68

So..69

Part III..71

When Coyote Sings 73

Wild(er)ness 74

Heading South..75

In These Wintered Woods 76

The Slow Curve of Sun.....................................77

Over the Mountain 78

Desert Scent..79

Long Night Moon..80

Spring on Steens Mountain 81

The Old Road..82

By These Desert Springs....................................83

Begging Call..84

Passed the Cattle Guards 85

Wind 86

August Is A Waltz..88

Taste of Heat...89

Twilight Road 90

Winter Mountain Snow.....................................91

Crow Moon 92

Cold As Coal 93

Blue Wilderness...94

Divinity..95

Blossom..96

Before Dinner 97

Sacred the Desert Tree..98

Where Grasses Bend 102

About the author 103

About EYEPUBLISHEWE 105

PART 1

March 2020

we were lovers once
and then
the end of the world happened

As They Count The Dead

in the shadows of a new york hospital
rows of refrigerated trucks squeeze
side by side like rotting lemons
to shelve the dead

dawn enters on outstretched wings
her feathered light casting ribbons
    of marmalade plums
        and overripe cherries across the sky
seagulls cry as they open the curtains
drawing in the day

Mimi German

Dusk

outside my window the rain drops hard

clacks the earth like worry beads

priestly trees sway like a thousand rabbis at the wall

nothing wails except the wind

prayers fold and tuck into origami prisms

float like kites toward the sky

i wonder who is left to do the bidding

to mind the castle when there is no one left

Containment

in the empty bowl

a white crowned pigeon

and a tattered feather

a bead lost from its rosary

a scalloped shell taken from its sea

a lover's footprint

washed away in the sand

a broken heart

the moan of an old man dying

the fading notes of an aria

a gray hair blows in from the east

a sun sets in a shard of mirror

a grifter wind lifts the bowl

tossing it to the ground

Mimi German

I Cannot Sleep

night presses its weight onto morning
like a well spent lover
colors petal the stem of sky

when you wake
there is no way to dream me
into water lapping at your feet

old roots finger the shoreline
of the lake yearning
for the soft body
of her wet sands

beneath the sagging breast
of a cypress tree a bird
sings into the silence
peeling back the husk of darkness for one more day

Inside This Abyss

the air is taut
    rife   with lonely

seconds batter the jetties of minutes
    jarring loose the urchins

across the canyon's rim tethered to nothing but july heat
    love walks the tightrope of longing

far below snakes hiss and rattle their tails
    in the sunlight seep

Mimi German

Sea Winds

on this bed of billowing sails

on a sea of mortal miles

how long can love last

Resembling A Dead Weed

i'm losing all my leaves

soon   i will resemble a dead weed

it appears that spring is here

and yet   and yet   and yet

earth is dry   thirsty

annihilative

and death is airborne

my thoughts refuse order and meaning is a lost dog

i taste the soil from my fingers to remember where i am

and who is the dawn

a swing scrapes the air in a neighbor's yard

crow is my shadow like bruised fruit to the orchard's floor

even if i asked

you cannot walk the cracks of this wadi with me

Mimi German

Time Immeasurable

i remember time

achingly slow but persistent

silent

curling its way into my body

dark with flecks of red and yellow

the gnarl of a thousand years

now of memories and your almost inaudible moan against the

arch of my pelvis

Indigo

in this indigo light

i am a rock broken

searching the layers

for the sounds of the sea

Mimi German

Adrift

how quickly the tide pushes us
farther
and farther
from any shore

Inside

it is quiet

everything is small

the fire in the wood stove

the night mouse   the moon

somewhere there is a sun

      and love

i sit on this couch

wondering if

clouds make sound as they pass through each other

      like the swish of fish deep in the sea

my hands look old

veins more transparent

under thinning skin

tired but no more linear

i am losing weight under this weight

it is hard to be hungry to hunger

through the scarcity of erased lines

tomorrow is a made up word

Mimi German

Love In The Hours

i remember then
the us   of you
me   a moonless night
unwinding on wandering curves
shadow trees   miles
back roads sleeping
horses in their barns
the slap of winter's air

my hands were cold   slipped
my fingers beneath your thigh
long stretches of contentment

the quiet of love   we'd crawl
into the worn
sheets scented in longing

        all this
peelings from yesterday's tangerine
the carpet is crooked yet warm beneath the feet of memory
the heart's flower blossoms unfractured
garden chimes wither but ring just the same

Where Grasses Bend

Fallen Fruit

in the dream

you reached out your arm to touch me

through the space of light years

through this galaxy of endlessness

as if fruit fallen from a tree

    could be returned to its branch

Mimi German

The Dark Bird

the dark bird sings
melancholy songs
into the refinery of night

Where Once A Jackal Walked

i remember things from this distance
like   that my wild is your spirit animal
i pace the jagged miles   sniffing each leaf
scratching the earth   for any scent
of life   of love

for the path beyond
these thistles
that leads me through
a thicket of darkness

and over crags of this monumental divide
longing screeches through empty canyons
where once a jackal walked
where once a vulture swooped
through the red veins of the valley under the gaze
of yellow asters
the path curves winding upstream
in the white waters rafting across my body

Mimi German

i rough the edges smooth then winnow soil from clay

i defy drought by thirsting on rays of the sun

but i cannot in all my wildness

find my way into you where i belonged

Where Grasses Bend

Hope

what is hope

in a plague

to live   to die

to skirt the ragged

crags

      of vacancy

and rusted tin can fires

i walk the miles through yesterdays

in rain

with hands unclasped

eyes fixed

to an unmarked trail

Mimi German

Searching For Air

the pause

the breath

the stops

the goes

the jang of this

Where Grasses Bend

In June, I Have Only Questions

it's been five months since your hands lips tongue eyes
my body burns like the bones of dying
forests ravaged by the emptiness of time
hours pass like a second hand in reverse

can one die by longing
or by letting go of air

magnolia blossoms still bloom
how the petals drop one
by one
no revisitation

petals fall
does anyone pick them up
where do they blow

Mimi German

Thirst

i thirst to sip

from your lips

once more

Burning Prayers

in the end

time is the great devourer

memories are mausoleum tatter

love thins on spindled threads

still   i image you into being

your bolts and screws

the rings of your tree

in the twisting root of morning's stretch

i originate you to the cob of caramelized paper

until the late train whistle blows

three blaring horns

short

long

then short

Mimi German

stars pollinate

dragging themselves across the palm

of darkness

my knees are dirty from crawling the ground

burning prayers crumpled and tossed

with each transiting shadow i bed down

with sorrow

waking to ash

and recollection trashed

Light Years

so many miles of seconds and light years of days since

Mimi German

Still Life

sky is moonlight gray
smells like lemons

earth collects afternoon rain
cottonwoods cast shadows

in the lonesome song
crow wings into the dark night

hearts of apple blossoms dot the trees
branches flex the empty pause

champagne hellebores bow
in resolute respect

from an old boot
a flower grows

no where
are the people

I Surrender

to the caravan and the orchid of fruit trees

to all the green steeples

to living   to death   to descent

to the bloom and the blossom of things

to your moan   i surrender

to the thresholds and to the cliffs

to the river's rushing waters

to the boulders that tumble and break at my feet

i surrender beholden

to no one but the earth herself

i lick from the leaf besotted with rain

to remember my name

in the crazy that bends in torrents in my head

to the torment of longing

i surrender to the shining star sun and to jupiter's moons

to the glorious cold of the dark desert night

to the cracks in the ceiling and the holes in the floor

Mimi German

to kindness

to scarcity

to the givers

to takers

and to love

o to love

Thoughts While Weeding During the Plague

my nails are getting long
dirt collects in them from the garden
plant seeds   weed my thoughts of you
in the deep sunshine of the plague
always there is you

found a marble beneath a mound of poppies
looked like the earth once looked
blue seas with green land mass
that was a time

tulips open   tulips close
blossoms beg   i beg for you
bees search for pollen
or die at your feet   quivering
for ever should always be two words

this is the garden speaking
we are speaking to you

Mimi German

this the same dirt they used
to bury my father
miles and miles of dirt
for the dead

an entire self is contained in a seed
then blown by the wind into the street and run over by a truck

there is life in this earth
that buries the dead
i lay my face on this earth and inhale

crow caws in a nearby tree
flaps his wings   lands in the scratch
looks at me sideways   deeper than the soul
there was a hole in the ground   in the ground   in the ground

Where Grasses Bend

Fermentation

how many days has it been
i have lost count
of the long nights

stalks are weathered
swirled in earth
and the tassels of herons

inside this density of darkness
i sit on this couch waiting
beneath the unbearable distance of stars

Mimi German

The Eighth Month

eventually the eyes hollow
lips turn into a crescent moon
we begin to see only the negative
space between leaves on the branch
shadows of what could have been

this is the lunch cart and the menu
too dangerous to eat
the sky sags into ism-less petals dried and powdered
life support is unplugged
in its silence   the tart laugh
on the settee of sangria suns

When The Ceiling Cracks

we are at deletion now

the weight of longing is three times

    the length of roots to its tree

language

    contracts

orgasms

    discontinue

breath

    is a hot commodity

fear is oversold and up for grabs

the ceiling is cracked and still

the meaning of all of this is nowhere

Mimi German

Morning Prayer

inside the petaled swell of spring
when willows bend from bursting buds
and honeyed waters tease the rocks
the naked breast of sloping banks
begs my prayer   a vagrant sky
let your tongue remember me

Of Love

the weight of love
is a stone bedded down
beneath layers of wet brown earth

tend to it
with blankets from winter's last leaves

feed it snowberries
    and the soft decay of time

indulge it with the ghostly dance of darkness
    in the erotic night

love tangles
    in the pines
        in the sap of bones
            and the salty bitters
of clarity

Mimi German

Caress its ice storms with honeyed breath
charm it like a snake slipping deeper into marshes

undress its nakedness with your teeth
braid it into plaits and weave them into your bed

but do not plead with it
      to stay

PART II

In This State

in this state
which state is the state
of the state of emergency

The Scenic View

O say can you see the burned out
burger barns that edge out the sky
where shadows of shackles obfuscate light
and sheds barely resemble houses resembling sheds
fields of flood plains now sop the cows so thick they bellow
then drown

above the crushed spine of a porch
the sign that said docs tavern is now
monty's tow and stow where antique dust is sold

america decays   'merica the beautiful
the buzz hum and flash of an electric billboard's broken lights
tells you that jesus saves   abortion kills   and
guns are for all and all are for one
blind is as blind sees here in the land of purple majesty
where lack of vision always wins

in the mobile home seep of this tumbleweed stew
sterilized wonder grows in the petri dish
the hills are steep and crumbling crackers
and the elk aren't crossing anymore

the scenic view looks out to hutchinson's shuttered
steel mill across the river
where the sunrise is a silhouetted ode to a dirge
and the wind is so strong it blows the seabirds sideways

Mimi German

in the wild west
cars drive into the ocean whose waves look like mud
all that's left are dark waters and the crystal clear dream
of receiving that lollipop some politician doled out to the rich

someone smashed the snake and left it on the trail
the mule with no name has gone off to find another sunset
cows converge on the side of the road where a truck with a
flat slowly rumbles by
jackals stole what would they could and the rest of
where   is scattered to the salty earth
no good for no one in the dawn's early light
where it's cold and here comes the rain

Where Grasses Bend

Barking At Crows

was looking for a trumpet player to blow

the muted notes of a poem

found a dog barking at crows instead

and a forest of ponderosa pines

and a few roundabouts that went round and round

two old indians sit in the burned out gas station

sucking down the heat

across the road the river flows a wild song

it's hot   too hot for the birds

dusty air pierces the breath

john deer bales row after row after row of misery

beneath the house on the hill that stalks

to the desert sail the trailers

a rusted red fender feathers the narrows

between road and crooked horizon

Mimi German

the road curves like love

horses eat at the trough unbridled and lazy

the foraging heat splinters skin like a dry fence post

hay bale of hell if you don't like how the willows weep

Where Grasses Bend

A Thousand Grains of Sand

amerikkka the dominatrix

empire of a thousand grains of sand

whose masters ink in the high heals of war whores

who circle jerk at the feast of landlords

while spilling slop bucket prayers

to the poor

amerikkka how necrotic your soul

your poets cringe in the wake of your obscenities

your rotted stench of henchmen

pillagers of lands once verdant and alive

your orchards of poverty

grow seeds of death

amerikka the illiterate

puritanical

and unsavory

you were never ready

to leave home

Mimi German

Poverty

poverty sits in a chair wearing a pair of blue shorts
shoelaces untied   hungry   waiting for no one in
particular and nothing at all   wears glasses missing a
lens seeing clearly the crack in the view

Apparition On a Park Bench

what was it

that unbalanced crouch on the bench

on the curbside of downtown

across from the fancy restaurant

serving up cocktailed delusions

that everything is fine

inside the red parka

there was no face

just an angled shadow

of a hard-on for the crumble

the smoked generosity of a wet dog

the hairpin laughter of mistrust riding the goat

grazing on this shoreline of poached lives

medium rare and dripping from the clasp

Mimi German

The Weight of Rain

the weight of rain is heavy

on flowering petals

so tenderly falling

9833 N. Willamette Blvd

we start our walks   my dog and i
visiting the driveway with the cat splayed out
like an unraveled wreath
the neighbors thought she was malnourished
and kidnapped her for a week

nothing really strives to live anymore
existence seems all the rage
dreams are soulless in the black and white din of the tv
we walk this long highway paved with no mercy
daydreams sprout like weeds
while poets tangle in the intractable wildness
of a star blazing peyote sky

to all the priests and all the paupers
sideline sitters and head bowers
traversers of sorrow sealed in lament
stilt walkers clomping for the deity of the day
to the kings and queens of cornhole
and crashers of the party
may you enjoy the broken lilt of decay

Mimi German

no matter how you try

the crow will forever never be the raven

the insolent sow never the milk dripping cow

in the parched hairs of the hour

we are woven into tatters

we walked by again   my dog and i

to see the cat   to share some love

but there was a sign in the driveway that read

neighbors   thank you for your concern

kitty had an autoimmune disease

was deeply loved

but has now passed on

Where Grasses Bend

Ferlinghetti's Interruption

she brought us coffee in the rain
and later   with another round
in pink pajamas and slip-on slippers and a book
she began to read
ferlinghetti's   *i am waiting*

we turned down the volume of the livestream
on death and dying at the end of the world
in order to hear   between the silence   the words
for anarchy   and   *rebirth of wonder*

i witnessed this pink bird in flight
arms waving with each line inside this heavenly shelter
her voice trumpeting to the heavens louder with each line

i am waiting
for the lost music to sound again

and

i am waiting for a way to be devised
to destroy all nationalisms
without killing anybody

i could hear the gentle spatter of spring rain on the driveway
and the words
unpremeditated art   making all things clear

Mimi German

and then my tears like petals fell for
the fleeing lovers
whom I would
embrace   indelible   perpetually and forever

Rosh Hashanah 5783

beneath the cracked bricks of bridges
     misery shelters from the sun
         stars stumble

truth is thinner than hunger
     hungrier than bread
         meaning is meaningless in the yarn

derelict vision hangs from the line
     the clerk of soul inventory
is crashed out on the floor
         honor is ash in a war torn street

is this how the world ends
     for whom have i been good
         a dispassionate rain falls

Mimi German

The Women Screamed

the chemicals i need

to feed my progeny

are no longer on the shelves

About That Toilet on Lombard

on the thoroughfare swollen tin sardines crest the crush of plastic bags then roll the winds of empty dreams between north or south rounding the edges of east or west along the silt of a crosswalk sits a drunk pigeon leaning on a tilting toilet for the ne'er do wells the everyday speeds by the broken locks and flapping doors screeching to a halt before hitting oversized wooks riding stolen bicycles from last year's october's surprise these are the incorporated sounds and images of the situation room inside the red walls of the roadside shit collector they call a toilet

the corner autumn turns to somber morning knows the stark the stark of stark the stark naked branches are coming to pillage the stark dream state of the forgotten

a mister and missus walk past the shitter they turn their square toward the sky in a vain attempt to fill the slatted empty boards of their silhouette cars chug by the toilet whose sign reads toilets are a human right churning the stench of poverty into tiny chocolates for the wealthy to place beneath next month's christmas tree fucking christ and his leftover loaves in the meantime this one girl the one with the buckskin hair who lived no where was lifting smiles from the passersby

Mimi German

she sold them each for a buck or a blow job   on the curb a
pigeon sits among the countless crows   white bread crumbs
skirt the highway of the unknown and never met   shadow
stoners beg to the dangling chad of night as blue as black is
blue   to reform tomorrow   to bask the day away in the
sunshine filled with poppy juice and all the drippings   the
twilight the dream cream sweet jim beam   that reminds me of
the time   when there was a time   now the gristle just hangs its
pride upon the fog of the lost shimmer   vacancy in the mind
of an amnesiac   the hours dim over this crosswalk   this parade
of pedigrees   two bit house thieves boot lickers and losers   its
all ever been about who could nab the hatchets   down for the
dogging   dodging the light   drowning

in the impenetrable suffocating toxicity of light   lost in flight
these birds of paradise   lost   in the listless gait of afternoon
shadows and the low tides of hours   we walk the wadi inside
the traveling dust bowl   the half starved are heralded as the
bottom of the barrel on the shoreline of despair

In America the Beautiful

the water's dirty man

you know what i mean

the stench not even a mother could pretend to love

like swill in the swale of a beached bloated whale

a cistern of stink like the sow of a politician let loose

in a sty of flies

yeah the water's dirty alright

too dark to see reflection in the old gulley

where love like bark

peels from its tree

abandoned in a sandbox near the liquor store dumpster

Mimi German

On the Bridge

saints hustle sky for real estate
jumpers cast off into the reflection of the gray warbling sun
yesterday's moorings were impounded and circumstance
tangoes on the ringlets of a slippery deck
aces are spades and queens are rooks and kings
well no one ever needed the king
o the upturned wind
sidewalks root the footsteps of the dead
the ghastly weed of history ties its knot to clouds
diaphanous and free

Walking The Slope

i walk the muddy rutted slope
past the trash pile the neighbors left
past the wild winter grasses loping eerily
in bough breaking winds
past the broken wheel of the crooked cart
the hop along snag of the half smile fence
the tatter of the torn

an unremarkable stone with the lean of aside
i walk this slope where worms hide for cover
and the almost of hail never comes
a girl tries to burn her footprints in the fire

you   worn as the rest
resume raking up the trash left behind
in someone else's oblivion and sweeter dream

no leaves hum
a barren stand of oaks grow bored
the calligraphy of stars tattoo the helmet of the crooked
heavens
a meadowlark sings a song so sad to no one
snakes troll the outbound train

Mimi German

War

beneath the thickets

the clutter of war

we are drowning in our

dumplings

United States

unknitted and frayed

unwound

a worn sweater

unspooling

into darkness

like moonless whores

on a parisian night

Mimi German

Joy

he's feral in all the hours and twisted seconds

raw wood   the color of your rust stained drain

you want joy   he's not your guy man

the incessant scratch from cantankerous mouths

you want joy   i mean   real joy   good luck

walking that horizon line   and watch out

for the crack somewhere left of center beyond the high heeled

sentiment of bourgeois ambition   his words belong   etched

into dirt beneath a rock

you want to know joy   joy is a low cut blouse lapping up the

bitter scent of shadows folding into the sagging cleavage of a

calving iceberg

joy   unprotected from the unprotected

the crisscosser of streets   an american failure

The Teapot

when the teapot falls from its hearth

it does not wait or wonder where

is the hand that will pick it up

to return it to the water

Mimi German

Night

is the stoned moan of poverty

and the song of a thousand frogs

it is an efficiency apartment for a fleeting dream

a star bordello

where a dark angel rides a gazelle

night is the owl

measuring the distance between here to there

night is wilderness collecting its thoughts

darkness the weight of a fugue

carousel of mourning

and the delivery truck of day

After the Protests

i've traveled into the cow of this day
smoked the verifiable roadkill stink of yesterday
picked the quills stuck to tar
for the holy beaded rucksack of later

blood has hardened in the dry
birds clamor for breath between tear gas blasts
we're in a one shoe on and a scuffing skiff
sail's up slashing at the stale

toy horses tied to the curb snort in fear
poverty paces as bedlam bellows
while the heavy black boot
makes fringe of my heart

Mimi German

Martyrs

in the early morning hours

when the sun clings morning to her skirts

rise   o' yesterday's ghosts

whose memories sequin the path in shimmering light

so the rest of us might see

I Kali

you didn't think you were going to meet i kali on the road yet
there she was   eyes blazing legs spread shooting her fire her
steaming flame into you and you are stunned immobile
wanting so much to run but not even a where to turn   lost in
the depth of her eyes her heart her pussy   all was open all
revealed and reviled   i kali wants you   i kali will not hurt you
but i kali will destroy you   come along for the ride boy   you
can't leave   you can't even move   look at you frozen in your
fear   you lust for your mother your sisters your daughters your
ego   i kali sees you with your hard-on fear   come here she
commands i kali wants to breathe on you into you taste your
ego take it in her hand and stroke it before breaking it into
pieces shattering you into flames   into being   but you aren't
ready yet i kali has your balls in her hands her mouth her spell
grabs at your breath your teeth   you roar to be released but
she licks you instead with her tongue of fire   you try hard not
to be turned on but the flames lick across your thighs i kali
sees you   licks your face and fucks your mouth of memory
fading you of you and when you finally dissolve i kali wraps
you in flames and sends you into the living

Mimi German

So

so there's a hawk
a raven and an owl
all sitting on a snag

Part III

When Coyote Sings

when coyote sings
open all the windows
and listen to his song

Wild(er)ness

they say nothing
is out here   that here
is the middle

    of nowhere
but here
exactly   here
you find your   where
on earth
your   who   you are   your   you

you are whole   here
where time is the existence of a sun
and a lizard who tells you that living is just luck

Mimi German

Heading South

morning's sombrero slurs across november's sky
clouds dance the sunrise of porcelain bones
an oversized flag on the weathered post blows
tattered meaningless and limp
cows palette the quiet stroke of autumn
we are starlings in a spray of quail

a barn cat sits in the middle of a field
wanting nothing more than nothing
in the wind   notes of distance
it's feeding time at the trough
where some get a lot but most get nothing

here   it's all mule skinner or the saddle up that drives the
compass west
sugar mints or caramels   this or that
that or this   ratta tat and ratta tat tat
cat in a field or a man in a hat
and the water dish has frozen

In These Wintered Woods

threaded to this ground

like tired blades of grass wet with winter

i am anchored

weathering

i am bark

then kindling

i am soil warmed beneath the unkempt circle

where the pregnant doe sleeps

here in the solitude of these old oaks

i lie still

     listening

Mimi German

The Slow Curve of Sun

in the dark tea of spring
brush and peat

time knocks
seeping

i cannot strain decay
like darning a cloak
or untangling braids of moss

the push broom scrapes
leaf from stalk

nothing grows wild
in the bitters

Over the Mountain

the trees change as the road grows long
the etch on bark where mosses grift
the cling of snow to root and rock

i watch the miles as we drive away from the city
to our home in the desert wilderness

raven eats the carcass of the roadside dead
the mountain looms in the past of a mirror
through the charred lands of yesterday's fires

rivers gather then turn like snakes into desert
woodlands to grasslands and fir to pine
here nothing is homeless

as we near the pueblos
beyond the worn lookouts and rumbling cattle guards
how beautiful the stark

moonlight greets us golden as straw before chiseling
into day
twilight brambles into the blush undressed
nothing here is forever

Mimi German

Desert Scent

it took seven days of desert immersion
to emerge in the scent
of desert of warm springs mud and yesterday's hot springs
with defined discernment between the sweet tin air
of rabbit brush against the warmth of summer's sage

the use of dreams are a spur of tumbleweed
vultures swirl in threes swooning over the dead
owl drops a feathered bed for a rabbit's jaw to land

we rake up the day in its remaining hours
foraging thoughts to share with stars
mountain blue bird hawks her beauty
raven backs and forths above and then below
stalks a desperate field mouse

such horrendous beauty in the wild
winds hurl curses from the mountains
down into the valley
into the rush of utter silence
as if all life ceased like the song of the frog
when a snake is near

Where Grasses Bend

Long Night Moon

long night moon

blue desert sea

a mountain stands

Mimi German

Spring on Steens Mountain

~~ o the sparse trees   the split trees   the half trees and the burrow trees
the one arm trees and the old crag trees   o the lone tree ~~

in the afterbirth of winter

we rejoice at last and open the windows wide

to breathe a deeper breath of sky

winter's paper grasses turn to fertile stalks of green

snow still clings to mountain crags and peaks

the songs of coyotes fold fields to clouds

and on the open slope of thighs

spring rides in unbridled

velvet auburn robes swath the new born fawns

wild flowers and balsa root shake their blossoms loose

to remind us what it is to earth ourselves

in such tambourine divinity

redwing blackbirds sweep the tongue of sagebrush fields

rabbit peaks from his namesake brush

we drink the running waters in pronghorn country

The Old Road

we the unbound

roll up the fences

walk the dusty wind of the old road

bluff for the view

lizard and sage

paintbrush magpie and lupine

pueblos peak and range

we are desert people now

who live with the dirt

inhaling the wind of ages

the soil of nomads

songs of ghosts

Mimi German

By These Desert Springs

i have learned the scent of sky
    and the taste of coming rain
can sing the song of the tired owl
    in the grove where willows sway

i hear the stars pluck midnight's dark
    and dance the quake of aspen leaves
i breathe the tolling beat of thunder from these hills
    and in these desert springs i bathe
    in praise of both the living
    and reverence for the dead

my feet are made of woven rushes
    in my dream still wet from water's breath
inside the furrowed bark of a stand of stately elms
    i place my fingers finding comfort
    in this desert i call home

Begging Call

today i prune the desert lilac
careful not to cut new shoots
where green leaves sprout
for some impossible future

to survive is an act of defiance
in the constant radiance
the deluge of desert's heat
to discern the living branch from the dead

nature is brutal
yesterday i dragged a dead coyote
off the middle of the road
hit so hard his entrails unraveled
and stuck as if glued to the melt of highway tar
i placed him in the sage brush for the vultures to consume
a feast a vulture would relish

i put down my pruners to listen to the wind
sometimes the screech of a hawk is not a hawk at all
but the begging call of an owlet
yearning for food or its mother
to protect her for another day

Mimi German

Passed the Cattle Guards

the yellow dash of staccato lines
suck and curl twisting around the wheel
into the twirl of summer heat

all the birds left the state on a yesterday like today
the lolligagging sky is an open casket for the wind

out on the far away beneath the scorching sun
a tree stands alone in its swank
tourmaline flowers cling to it as if
hope for survival is real

in this heat the clouds are a tree
the tree is a horse
and the horse is a shadow
of the craggy desert sage

nothing rebels
the king bull sleeps
drunk ants attack the dusty path
looking for mister bojangles
and the mantis prays to be saved
from the salvage yard of the living

Wind

you can tell the weather out here by the way the wind
breathes or
is as perfectly still as a dead dragonfly stuck to a leaf

the wind is trickster

thunder rolls like quarter notes across the dry

onto the basin floor while hiked up pleats of virga clouds

defy the urge to ground

even the lizard waits now

for the thrum to wet his spine

we all wait

coyote calls to another and then another

through the stillness of thick air

Mimi German

grasses agitate above the curve

while lightning flares the span

a sea of clouds traverse the sky road

sticking to the mountain's range

not I or raven or mouse or owl can tell

when the rain will land

Where Grasses Bend

August Is A Waltz

the desert is blue
paper thin and fragile
like ghosts in the owling winds
that wrap this house in parchment memories
and dust from the pueblos

i watch her like a hawk from sun to moon
i'd say like a raven but the ravens are too busy
for such idling

sometimes she is a rhumba
but in august always a slow waltz

Mimi German

Taste of Heat

the mothership is seared

crisped to the crunch

the stetson hat strays its wick

no one's going no where

beyond that creamsicle horizon

miles to giddyap but not today

unless you're an ornery raven

or a fly looking for something dead

water's on the loose like cattle

you could grease the saddle in the scent of dry grass

this long dusty road is a boot hole in the desert sink

Twilight Road

the gall of it

rats ride the dusk raft

cling to the wind

the sagebrush scrag

ghosts rabbit like moths

fluttering into the wind's shield of light

and the yellow flowers

hide in the shallows

cheap tin roofs flap offbeat

into long hollow

Mimi German

Winter Mountain Snow

winter mountain snow
a juniper births
on windy rock

Crow Moon

at 6 am we rise with the dawn
of this our second crow moon
we feed the fire and then the dog
then wait and watch for the breaking band
of light delineating day from night

december's morning frosts
have turned a quiet golden mat
soon the sun will shake awake the temple ghosts
their chant and chilly moan
where winter's hold so slowly lifts
and pale of wind-bent grasses drift
against this priestly ledge of mountain
where jagged shadows comb

over in the valley not far from this desert scene
geese clatter the canals pecking earth for insect and seed
snow rims canyon peaks and the bare burned bones of trees
a cold song blankets the walls as winter roams these fields
hunting down the sun not missing us at all

Mimi German

Cold As Coal

the days darken with the desert's dead and dying
and our morning bed is cold as coal
autumn's temple oxidized to dust
leaves   the color of cayenne
crumble to a carnelian crust

upon the dusk rests a red throated sky
song birds preen the souse under threaded braids of rain
snow marks like chalk the fall of summer's thornless rose
and now the sun   a burned out brick
blows gales of ash into the stove

the day rickets for one last luster
my mother calls wondering why i am
here in this wildness of wilderness
a cattle truck trudges up the hill
i pour more wine into my glass
counting quail in the quiet before the onslaught of winds

Blue Wilderness

like the last person alive
she yearns for the last peony
in a drunken field of wildflowers

clouds graze on raven scented air
aware of darkness colluding with light
assembling the appendage of dawn

but morning patina billows blue
desert blue   lonesome blue

> shadows
>
> silhouette
>
> mountainsides
>
> root

on weathered rock late autumn heaves
and tumbles across the stutter
exhausted grasses wet from a moonless rain
fold toward winter's coming
> where only truths grow acres long

Mimi German

Divinity

i wake   inside the divinity   of you

Where Grasses Bend

Blossom

in your palm
sunday is wet

yearning burns
in the wood stove

burst open !

yellow fuchsia
bellows spring

Mimi German

Before Dinner

the sun like a god blazed through winter's window

you read to me the last poem

in harjo's new book

i loved you more

than i have ever

loved

Sacred the Desert Tree

across from the old school house
we stood in a graveyard of trees

i could hear the death rattle
of falling ancient willows

a thunder that breaks
humans from their gods

surrounding the desert
high above the playa
the mountain sheep bray on rimrock
delirious and unhinged from summer's dry bones

coyote slumbers
scarred earth hardens
a dream reflects in a jackrabbit's eye
sounds of water taste like rock
these things are sacred too

Mimi German

lone juniper stands
beneath scorching sun
a sentinel

shadows of the fallen whisper
faltering into night
witness divinity
tilling the dark of dawn

bathe unmarked, naked!
in the soft tongue of sagebrush

her scent wet with waking

holy is the conjurer of life
purveyor of death
inside the wooden wheel
on the worn and rugged path

Where Grasses Bend

and holy this earth
rivulets of blue of red of wine
in this silence of the desert
where dead trees lie
spring lifts its winter skirts

every thing is heard

the rancher speaks in moons
and stars graze in desert sands

holy is the wild
no longer that of man
but of Love !

Mimi German

of poets and wanderers
riders of unsaddled horses

holy holy holy be their names
a bouquet of bones thrust
into the stumble
waking us into the infancy
of day

Where Grasses Bend

winter winds blow down from the pueblos

gales of snow encircle the house

like ghosts   hungry

pressing their urgency

against these mortared walls

inside i write poetry

warm   beside the stove

Mimi German

About the author

Mimi German is a poet and subversive artist dividing her time between life in the wilderness of Oregon's Steens Mt. and the urban strife of Portland, OR. Her first book of poetry, Beneath the Gravel Weight of Stars, was released in 2022 weaving her experiences as an advocate for unhoused Portlanders through poetry.

Born a wanderer, Mimi left Philadelphia for NY in '82 for college. It was in NYC during the Reagan Administration that her first of a few non-violent disobedient arrests occurred. After college she joined the peace movement, Shalom Achshav (Peace Now), in Israel arriving just before the first Palestinian uprising. After returning to the US, Mimi split time between Cambridge, MA and Halifax, Nova Scotia eking together money through nude modeling and as a musician busking on the streets of Halifax and Cambridge.

In 1995, Mimi hit the road to head west to Oregon where she still resides. In 1997, Mimi was arrested again, this time on Shoshone land in Nevada with the late Chief Corbin Harney protesting against a proposed uranium dumpsite.

In 2011 after the Fukushima nuclear disaster, Mimi started an international group called RadCast which documented citizen radiation readings post-Fukushima, from around the globe. She was often asked to speak about the reality of radioactive toxicity around the globe on national and international talk shows. She was a frequent guest on Michael J. Ruppert's show, The Lifeboat Hour and had a special weekly spot for radiation readings on Thom Hartman's show. After many years after it was clear that we as a society would never be rid of nuclear power, Mimi chose to act locally instead by doing direct support for unhoused people in Portland, OR. She is still doing that work today. Mimi is co-teaching an ongoing poetry workshop with unhoused poets at the offices of Street Roots, a newspaper written by the Portland unhoused community.

Where Grasses Bend is Mimi's second book of poetry that was written from the start of the pandemic through today. The poems are about loss, longing, humanity, and the regeneration of Love as it presents itself in the wilderness of Oregon.

Mimi's poetry has been published in the New Generation Beats Anthology 2022 and in the National Beat Poetry Foundation's, Remembering Jack Kerouac On His 100th Birthday. In 2023, Mimi was honored with the title of State of Oregon Beat Poet Laureate.

Her poems have also been published in the UK in International Times (IT), Steel JackDaw Magazine and in the US, Sublunary Review, The Hopper Magazine, The Mantle, Three Line Poetry (Vols. 51/52), New Verse News and was a finalist in The Poetry Box and The Hopper for best chapbook manuscript. Her poems can also be found in the testimony files of Portland City Council sessions between 2017-2020. For more information MimiGermanPoetry.org.

About EYEPUBLISHEWE

Eye publish ewe (EYEPUBLISHEWE) is a brand new publishing company, founded in San Francisco. Art, music, video, poetry, and other literature will find inclusive shelter here. Quality work produced by the artists' hearts, minds, and souls rather than commercial interests will have this as a home. All are welcomed with open minds and hearts and eyes to the future. Together we will publish art for humanity's sake.

EPE titles

The Green Notebook: Poems on Family, Relationships, Spirituality, Self-Enquiry, Recovery, ACA, Disruption, Death, Walking Through the Mirror, and Cats by **John Angell Grant** ISBN: 979-8-9870259-6-3

The Whole Existential Novel: The Journey from the Dark Side of the Rainbow to Satchidananda by **Dane Ince** ISBN: 979-8-9870259-0-1

Good Grief...Please!: A Dialogue with Death and Life by **Tish Ince** ISBN: 979-8-9870259-2-5

EPE titles
coming soon

A House Without Walls: Existential Journeys and Love Poems to Mexico by **Lesley Constable**

"Naturalzela del Amor" poems in Spanish and English by **Martin Del Toro Gutierrez**